new orleans

Arranged by Brent Edstrom

contents

T0071693

ISBN 978-1-4584-0600-2

7777 W. BLUEMOUND RD. P.O. BOX 13819 MILWAUKEE, WI 53213

Visit Hal Leonard Online at
www.halleonard.com

BASIN STREET BLUES

Words and Music by
SPENCER WILLIAMS

BLUEBERRY HILL

Words and Music by AL LEWIS,
LARRY STOCK and VINCENT ROSE

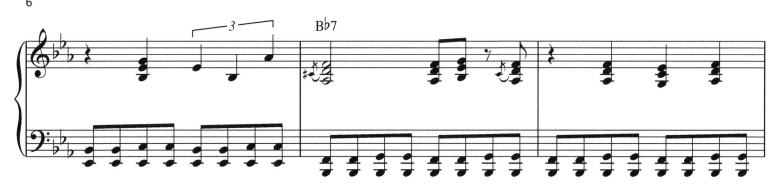

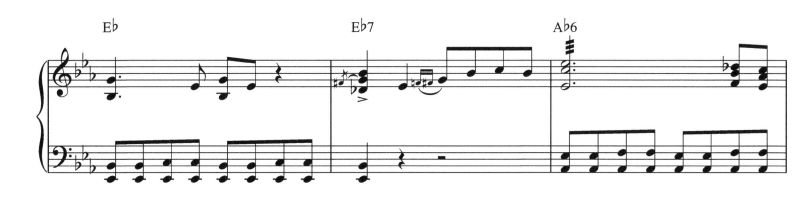

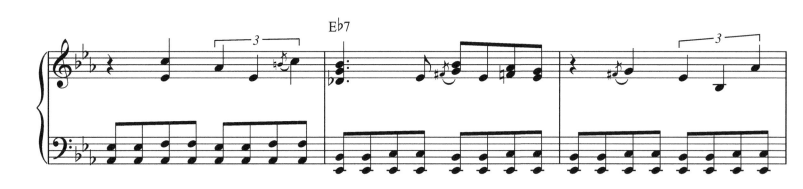

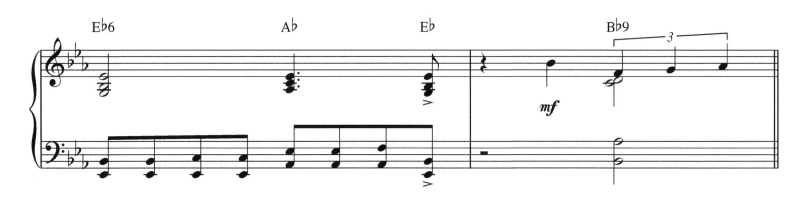

BIG CHIEF

By EARL KING

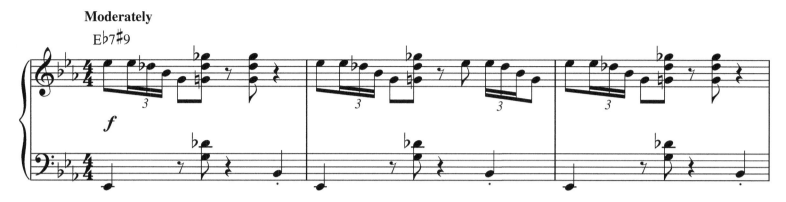

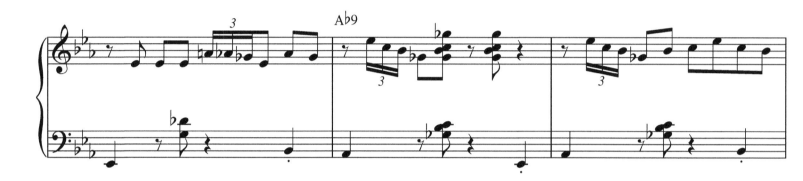

DO YOU KNOW WHAT IT MEANS
TO MISS NEW ORLEANS

Written by EDDIE DE LANGE
and LOUIS ALTER

FREEDOM FOR THE STALLION

Words and Music by
ALLEN TOUSSAINT

IKO IKO

Words and Music by ROSA LEE HAWKINS,
BARBARA ANN HAWKINS, JOAN MARIE JOHNSON,
JOE JONES, MARALYN JONES,
SHARON JONES AND JESSIE THOMAS

Moderately

HEY NOW BABY

By HENRY ROELAND BYRD

Rhumba

JAMBALAYA
(On the Bayou)

Words and Music by
HANK WILLIAMS

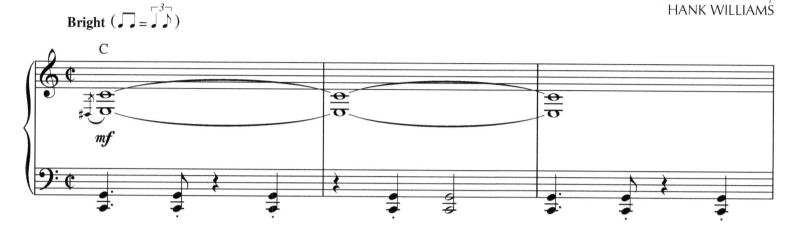

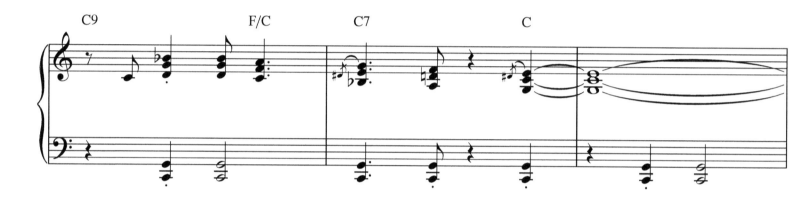

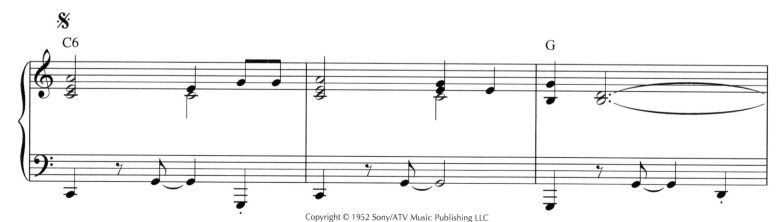

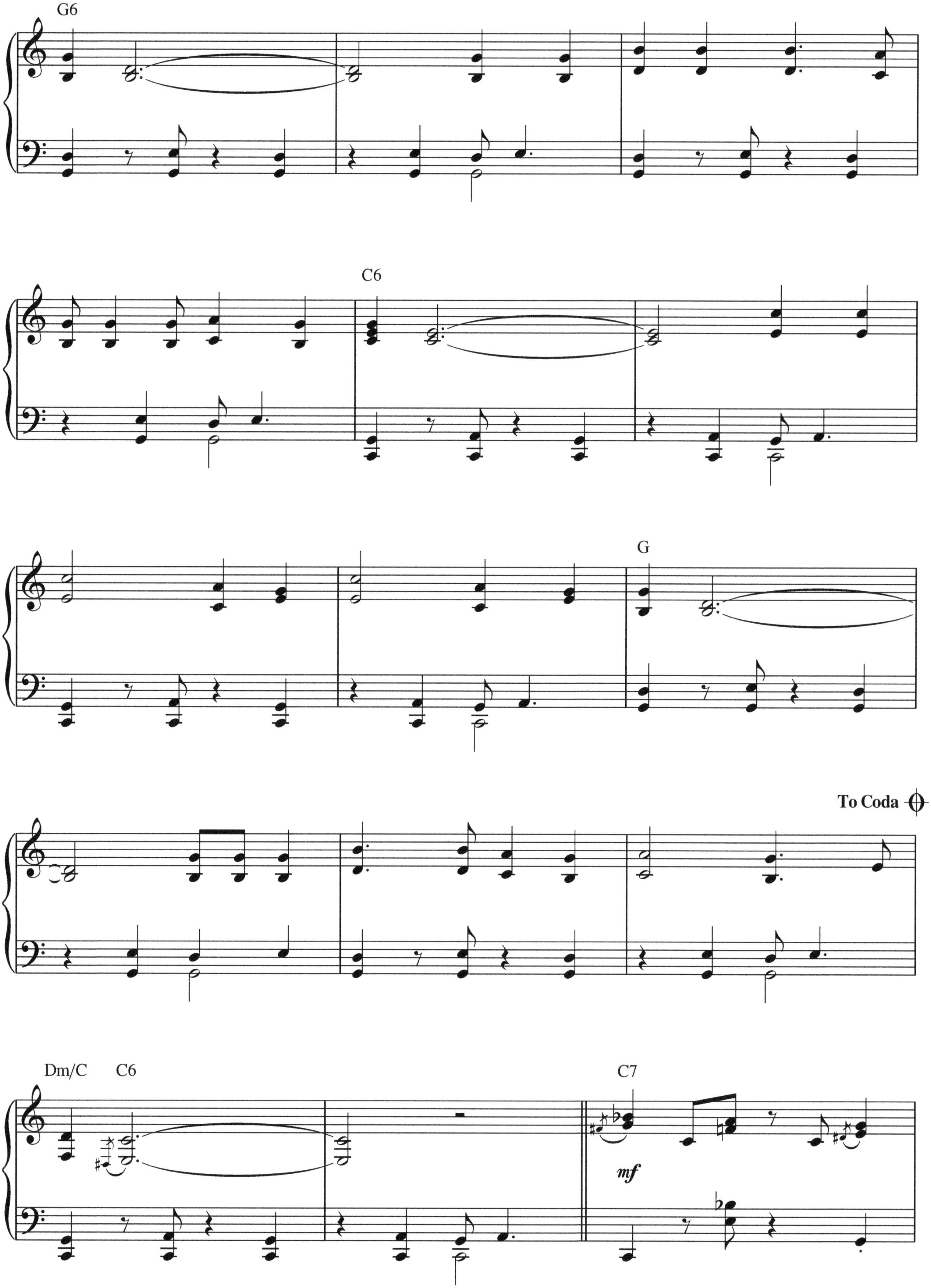
G6
C6
G
To Coda
Dm/C
C6
C7
mf

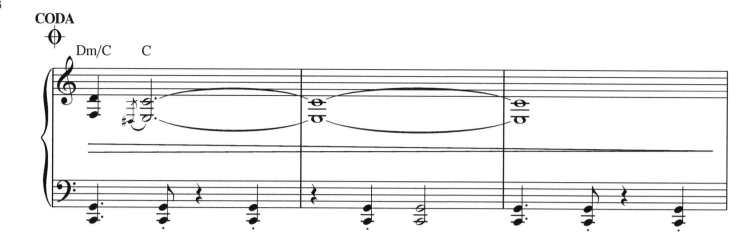

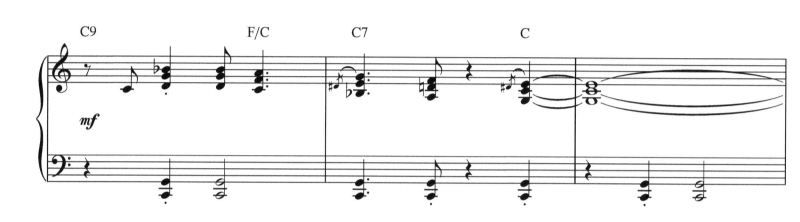

KING PORTER STOMP

By FERD "JELLY ROLL" MORTON

KANSAS CITY STOMP

By FERD "JELLY ROLL" MORTON

MARDI GRAS IN NEW ORLEANS

By HENRY ROELAND BYRD

Bright Rhumba

NEW ORLEANS BLUES

By FERD "JELLY ROLL" MORTON

OH ATLANTA

Words and Music by
WILLIAM PAYNE

THE PEARLS

By FERD "JELLY ROLL" MORTON

ON THE SUNNY SIDE OF THE STREET

Lyric by DOROTHY FIELDS
Music by JIMMY McHUGH

Medium Swing

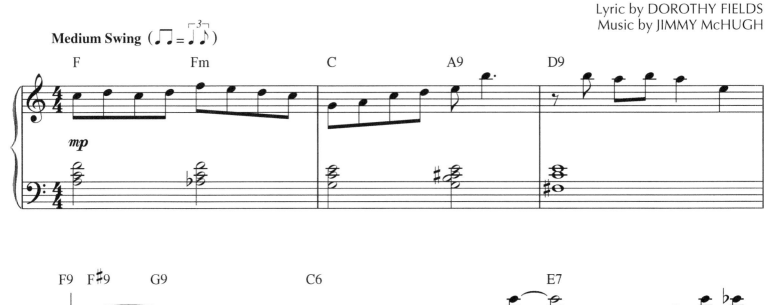

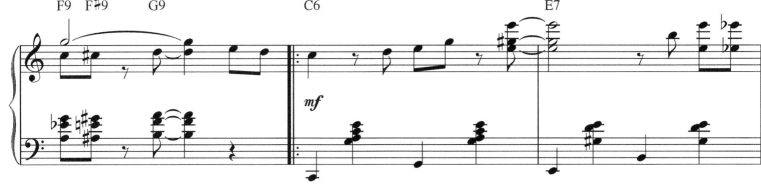

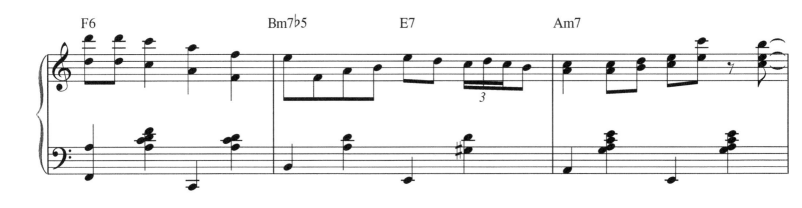

65

PIXIE

Words and Music by
JAMES BOOKER

Arrangement based on one by James Booker

TIGER RAG
(Hold That Tiger)

Words by HARRY DeCOSTA
Music by ORIGINAL DIXIELAND JAZZ BAND

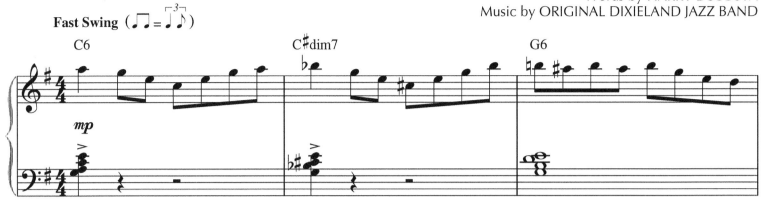

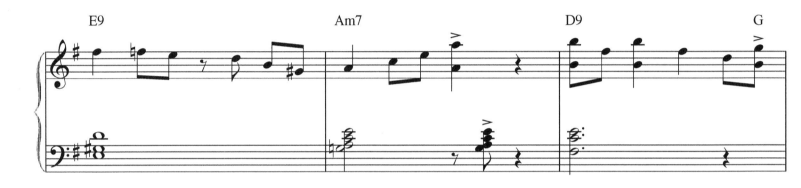

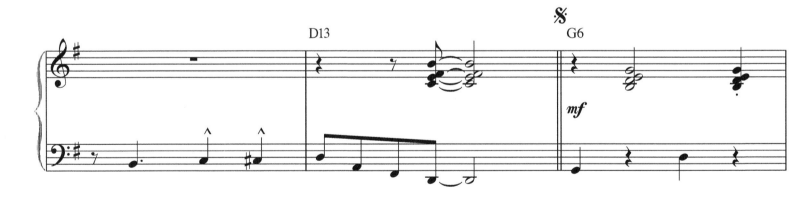

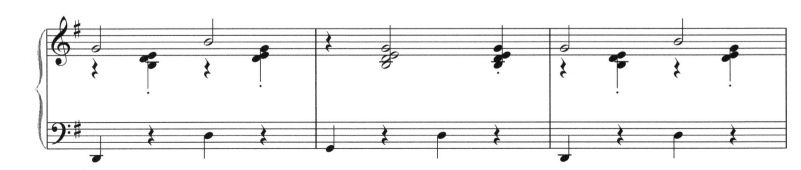

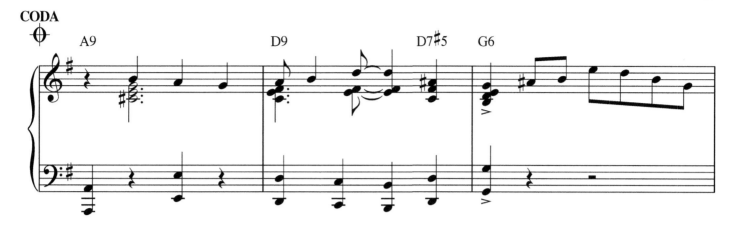

TIPITINA

By HENRY ROELAND BYRD

Moderate Blues

Arrangement based on one by Dr. John

YES WE CAN CAN

Words and Music by
ALLEN TOUSSAINT

Moderately fast

STARS AND STRIPES FOREVER

By JOHN PHILIP SOUSA